Picture Puzzles

PLACES & SCENES

igloo

igloo

Published in 2009
by Igloo Books Ltd
Cottage Farm
Sywell
NN6 0BJ
www.igloo-books.com

10 9 8 7 6 5 4 3 2 1

ISBN: 978-1-84817-492-4

Printed and manufactured in Singapore

Picture Puzzles
PLACES & SCENES

Picture Puzzles is created to test your powers of observation.
There are three types of puzzle in this book – spot the difference between two pictures,put a jumbled image in the correct order, or spot the odd one out of four images.

There are also four levels:
Novice, Wizard, Know it All and Mastermind, which have increasing levels of difficulty.
The Novice level has 6 changes for spot the difference, Wizard has 9, Know it All has 11 and Mastermind has 15. And if that isn't enough to challenge you, each puzzle has a time limit for you to beat!

HOW TO PLAY THE PUZZLES:

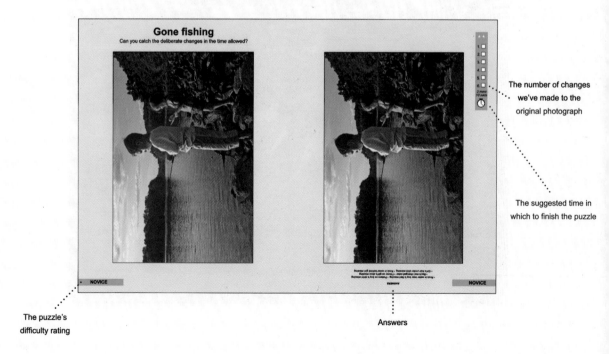

The number of changes we've made to the original photograph

The suggested time in which to finish the puzzle

The puzzle's difficulty rating

Answers

New York, New York

Spot the difference in this busy New York street scene.
There are 6 differences at Novice level.

NOVICE

★★

1. ☐

2. ☐

3. ☐

4. ☐

5. ☐

6. ☐

3 mins 10 secs

ANSWERS

• Color of panel on building • Words missing on red store sign
• Words missing on cab door • White lines on road missing
• Traffic signal missing • Illuminated sign missing

NOVICE

A day at the beach

Spot the differences at the beach.

★★

1. ☐
2. ☐
3. ☐
4. ☐
5. ☐
6. ☐

3 mins 10 secs

ANSWERS

- Strap on girl's arm missing • Flipper on far right missing
- Blue flipper different color • Hole in red flipper missing
- Blue strap on mask missing • Ridges on yellow flipper missing

Playtime

What differences can you see at the park?

★★

1. ☐
2. ☐
3. ☐
4. ☐
5. ☐
6. ☐

3 mins 15 secs

ANSWERS

• Tuft of hair missing top of child's head • T-shirt changed color
• Rivets on swing left-hand side missing • Vent on child's left-hand shoe missing
• Post on left-hand missing • Woman's bracelet missing

NOVICE

A walk in the park

Are the changes easy to spot?

NOVICE

★★

1. ☐

2. ☐

3. ☐

4. ☐

5. ☐

6. ☐

3 mins 10 secs

ANSWERS

- Saddle on bike missing • Large branch left-hand side missing
- Buttons on jacket of man's arm missing • Pattern on woman's jeans missing
- Man's right ear missing • Pile of leaves by man missing

NOVICE

A day out

It's fun at the park.

NOVICE

★★

1. ☐

2. ☐

3. ☐

4. ☐

5. ☐

6. ☐

3 mins 10 secs

ANSWERS

• Man's right shirt collar missing • Man's left shoe missing
• Child's jumper color changed • Child's badge on jeans missing
• Woman's broach missing • Woman's left-hand little finger missing

Yipee!

Can you beat the clock on this challenge and be a winner?

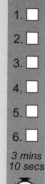

1. ☐
2. ☐
3. ☐
4. ☐
5. ☐
6. ☐

3 mins 10 secs

ANSWERS

• Palm tree missing frond • Old man missing watch
• Middle man t-shirt changed color • Man on right missing left eyebrow
• Man on left stripe on right sock missing • Cement in paving slab in middle missing

Visit the coral reef

There's a lot to see underwater.

★★

1. ☐
2. ☐
3. ☐
4. ☐
5. ☐
6. ☐

3 mins 10 secs

ANSWERS

• Yellow fish missing • Yellow fish different color
• Extra orange fish on rock • Flippers different color
• Extra ripples in water • Pink coral missing on rocks

Keep fit

Keep your observation skills fit with this challenge.

NOVICE

☆☆

1. ☐

2. ☐

3. ☐

4. ☐

5. ☐

6. ☐

3 mins 20 secs

ANSWERS

- Dog on left back paw missing • Man's tread on shoe missing
- Man's left ear missing • Man's stripe on short left-hand side missing
- Stripe on woman's shorts changed color • Dog on right tongue missing

NOVICE

Taken for a ride

Can you see the wood for the trees?

NOVICE

★★

1. ☐

2. ☐

3. ☐

4. ☐

5. ☐

6. ☐

3 mins 10 secs

ANSWERS

• Man's t-shirt changed color • Vent on helmet right-hand side top missing
• Strap on left-hand glove missing • Watch missing
• Left-hand foot missing • Branch on tree right-hand side missing

NOVICE

Fun at the fair

This challenge is a merry-go-round.

NOVICE

1. ☐

2. ☐

3. ☐

4. ☐

5. ☐

6. ☐

3 mins 10 secs

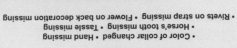

ANSWERS

• Color of collar changed • Hand missing
• Horse's tooth missing • Tassle missing
• Rivets on strap missing • Flower on back decoration missing

Reach the top

Can you reach the dizzy heights of beating the clock?

NOVICE

1. ☐
2. ☐
3. ☐
4. ☐
5. ☐
6. ☐

3 mins 15 secs

ANSWERS

• Cloud above head missing • Hat changed color
• Moustache missing • Shoe lace missing
• Shoe tongue changed color • Rock missing under large rock by shorts

NOVICE

Out of order

Can you place the pieces of this picture in the right order?

★★

50 secs

A B C D

NOVICE

ANSWER: D, C, B, A

Out of order

This street scene needs placing in the right order.

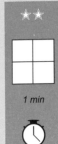

1 min

A

B

C

D

ANSWER: C, A, D, B

NOVICE

Gone fishing

Can you catch the deliberate changes in the time allowed?

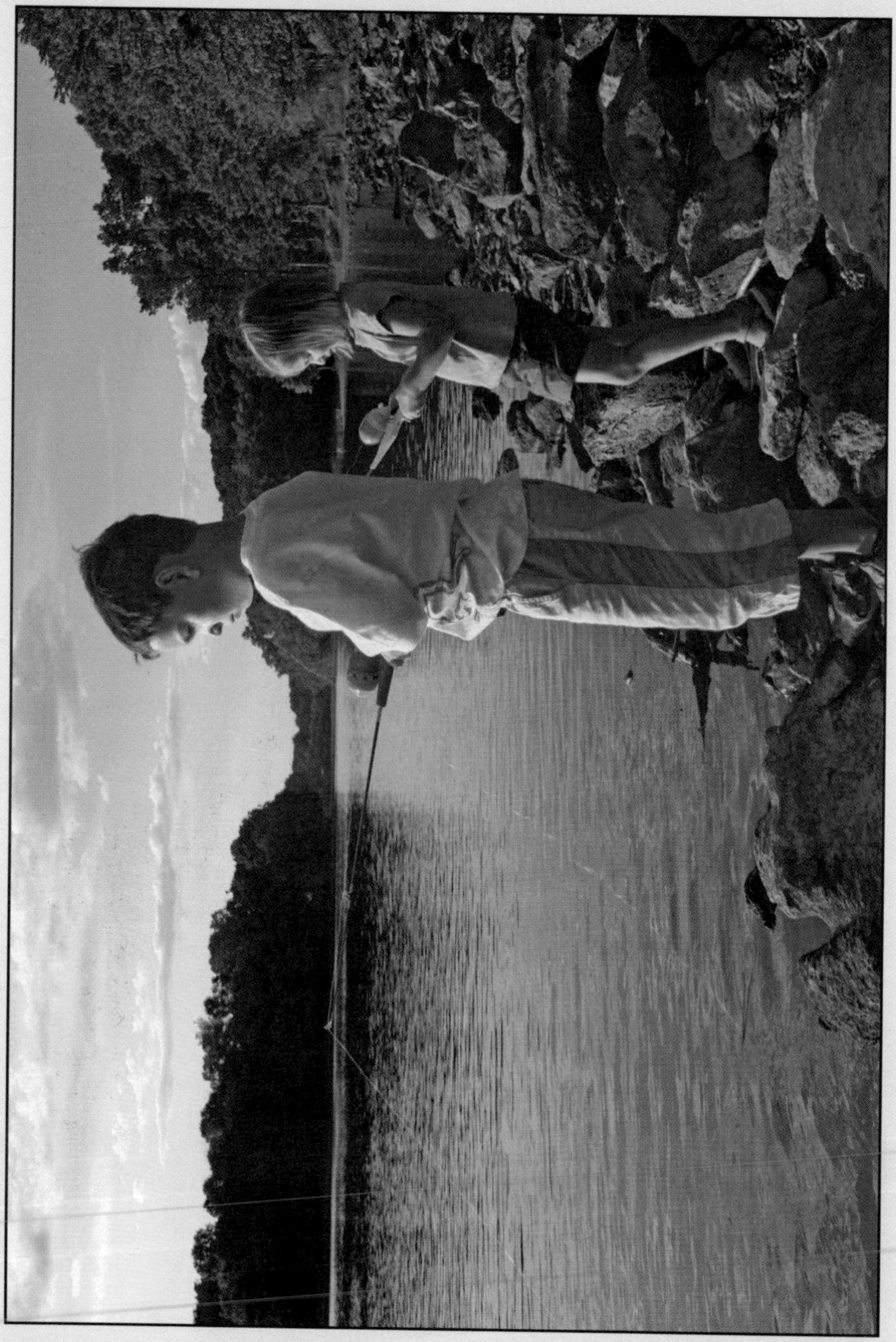

NOVICE

1. ☐
2. ☐
3. ☐
4. ☐
5. ☐
6. ☐

3 mins 10 secs

ANSWERS

• Rock in water near boy's feet missing • Pattern on boy's shirt missing
• Boy's reel changed color • Flower on girl's shoe missing
• Girl's hair under chin missing • Rock in water behind girl missing

NOVICE

Out of order

Don't jump! Place this picture in the right order.

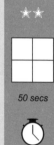

★★

50 secs

A B

C D

NOVICE

ANSWER: B, C, D, A

Out of order

What is the right order for this picture?
You need to be speedy.

50 secs

A

B

D

[redacted]

Rider's challenge

See if you can beat the clock on this one.

★★

1. ☐
2. ☐
3. ☐
4. ☐
5. ☐
6. ☐

3 mins 10 secs

[redacted]

[redacted]ERS

[redacted] • End of whip missing

[redacted]e stripe on horse's head wider

[redacted]Dogs tail missing

NOVICE

Ready, steady go!

Can you win the race against the clock?

★★

1. ☐
2. ☐
3. ☐
4. ☐
5. ☐
6. ☐

3 mins 15 secs

ANSWERS

• Number 2 missing • Sign in ambulance window missing
• Back wheel missing • Red V on helmet different color
• Extra shape on front bumper • Snow on edge of track missing

NOVICE

Thai market

There's lots going on at this fruit and vegetable market.

NOVICE

★★

1. ☐

2. ☐

3. ☐

4. ☐

5. ☐

6. ☐

3 mins
5 secs

ANSWERS

• Hat bigger • Pink coat different color
• Shadow on dock missing • Extra green hat on boat
• Extra piece of bamboo in foreground • Carving on back of boat on left missing

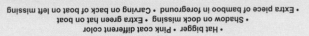

NOVICE

Head in the clouds

Is your head in the clouds on this puzzle?

NOVICE

NOVICE

ANSWERS

• Pink & white flower left-hand side missing • Belt loop missing
• Hair under neck missing • Mole missing
• Flower in hair changed color • Large white flower at front missing

3 mins 15 secs

6. ☐
5. ☐
4. ☐
3. ☐
2. ☐
1. ☐

★★

Taxi!

Can you see what's changed on this London cab?
There are 9 changes at Wizard level.

WIZARD

1. ☐
2. ☐
3. ☐
4. ☐
5. ☐
6. ☐
7. ☐
8. ☐
9. ☐

4 mins 20 secs

ANSWERS

• Cab steering wheel missing • Cab side indicator missing • Badge on door missing
• Man climbing into cab shirt cuff missing • Stripe on pavement missing • Bus number missing
• Cut off branch on tree missing • Woman behind cab door bag strap missing • Symbol on bus stop missing

WIZARD

Storytime

Spell out the changes between these two pictures.

WIZARD

1. ☐

2. ☐

3. ☐

4. ☐

5. ☐

6. ☐

7. ☐

8. ☐

9. ☐

4 mins 20 secs

ANSWERS

• Man's sideburn missing • Button on man's top missing • Man's top changed color
• Baby's top changed color • Woman's arm behind baby missing • Woman's ring missing
• Stripe on girl's top on right missing • Girl on right hair band missing • Girl on right mole on face missing

WIZARD

Keeping up appearances

Keep up with the neighbors by noticing what's changed.

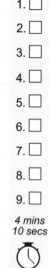

1. ☐
2. ☐
3. ☐
4. ☐
5. ☐
6. ☐
7. ☐
8. ☐
9. ☐

4 mins 10 secs

ANSWERS

• Door knocker missing • Door on left different color
• Molding at top of pillar missing • Railing missing • Handrail missing
• Extra flower on plant • Bike saddle missing • Doorbell missing • Frame in top right window missing

Start the barbecue

What changes have been served up here?

1. ☐
2. ☐
3. ☐
4. ☐
5. ☐
6. ☐
7. ☐
8. ☐
9. ☐

4 mins 15 secs

ANSWERS

- Curl missing from man's forehead • Stripe missing from man's top on back
- Stripe missing from man's sleeve • Piece of chicken missing from end of kebab on plate
- Large black stain missing from bottom of BBQ • Onion under BBQ missing • Can changed color
- Button from sleeve missing from man on right • Seam on jeans missing

WIZARD

Odd one out

Which picture is different from the rest?

A. ☐
B. ☐
C. ☐
D. ☐
1 min

A

B

C

D

ANSWER: B - Windsurfer missing

Odd one out

Which snowy scene is different?

A. ☐

B. ☐

C. ☐

D. ☐

50 secs

A

B

C

D

ANSWER: D - Street lamp missing

WIZARD

Manhattan skyline

Spot the changes in this famous skyline.

1. ☐

2. ☐

3. ☐

4. ☐

5. ☐

6. ☐

7. ☐

8. ☐

9. ☐

4 mins
10 secs

ANSWERS

• Flag on bridge missing • Yellow shirt different color • Bottle on far right missing
• Building in center wider • Top of brown skyscraper missing • Support on freeway missing
• Girl's bowl of salad missing • White fork missing • Skyscraper left of center missing

WIZARD

Thames at night

Take a close look at Tower Bridge, London.

WIZARD

1. ☐
2. ☐
3. ☐
4. ☐
5. ☐
6. ☐
7. ☐
8. ☐
9. ☐

4 mins 10 secs

WIZARD

ANSWERS

Barge missing • Crane missing • Middle window 1st tower 3rd level missing
2nd spot light middle support missing • Gherkin building missing • 2nd tower 2nd spire missing
Square at bottom 2nd tower missing • 3rd support right-hand side missing • Right-hand window last small tower missing

A trip to Paris

This bridge in Paris, France, has 9 changes. Can you find them?

WIZARD

1. ☐

2. ☐

3. ☐

4. ☐

5. ☐

6. ☐

7. ☐

8. ☐

9. ☐

4 mins 10 secs

ANSWERS

- Window missing from top of dome • Statue of lion left-hand side missing
- Sign under bridge missing • Reflection on water under bridge missing • Sword on 1st gold statue missing
- 6th lampost on bridge missing • 2nd golden statue wrong way round
- Gold button on bridge missing underneath 3rd lampost from right • Garland bridge suppost missing from right-hand side

WIZARD

Life's a beach

You can jump for joy, if you find the changes.

WIZARD

1. ☐

2. ☐

3. ☐

4. ☐

5. ☐

6. ☐

7. ☐

8. ☐

9. ☐

4 mins 10 secs

ANSWERS

- Man on left wristwatch missing • Girl on left hair missing • Man in middle shorts changed color
- Girl on right wristband missing • Man on right belt buckle missing • Man on right ring missing
- Cloud missing • Surf on far left missing • Part of woman's red hair missing

WIZARD

Sink or swim

Can you find the changes in time?

1. ☐
2. ☐
3. ☐
4. ☐
5. ☐
6. ☐
7. ☐
8. ☐
9. ☐

4 mins 15 secs

ANSWERS

• Mountain ridge on left missing • Oar of man back left missing
• Vent in helmet of woman on left middle missing • Life jacket of man front of left changed color • Piece of webbing missing
• Man back right yellow pocket missing • Man middle right wristwatch missing
• Man front right helmet changed color • Oar underneath man front right missing

WIZARD

The art of Zen

Fine tune your powers of observation.

1. ☐
2. ☐
3. ☐
4. ☐
5. ☐
6. ☐
7. ☐
8. ☐
9. ☐

4 mins 5 secs

ANSWERS

• Statue of bird on roof missing • Branch in top right missing • Doorway on top floor missing
• Part of fence missing on middle floor • Rock in water missing • Small branch on right of tree missing
• Part of roof missing • Wooden pillar on ground floor missing • Clouds behind trees missing

WIZARD

Out of order

Take the plunge and put this picture in the right order.

50 secs

A

B

C

D

WIZARD

ANSWER: D, A, C, B

1. ☐
2. ☐
3. ☐
4. ☐
5. ☐
6. ☐
7. ☐
8. ☐
9. ☐

4 mins 10 secs

WIZARD

ANSWERS

• Boat on lake missing • Path in woodland missing • Goggles different color
• Island behind head missing • Dial on wrist missing • Part of glove missing
• Strap on chest missing • Red cord on right of chest missing • Stripe on leg different color

Camping out

How long will it take to find these changes?

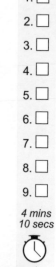

1. ☐
2. ☐
3. ☐
4. ☐
5. ☐
6. ☐
7. ☐
8. ☐
9. ☐

4 mins 10 secs

ANSWERS

• Branch at front of pic missing • Large rock left-hand side missing
• Rock by tent missing • Trainers by tent missing • Flames in fire missing
Man's coat changed color • Head of guitar missing • Cushion changed color • Leg of seat missing

It’s a winner

Are you going to be the first to finish?

1. ☐
2. ☐
3. ☐
4. ☐
5. ☐
6. ☐
7. ☐
8. ☐
9. ☐

4 mins 5 secs

WIZARD

ANSWERS

- Whip missing from rider on left • Goggles missing from helmet of 2nd rider
- Horse mask changed color on 1st horse • Stripes missing from bandage of leg of 1st horse
- Mark missing from head of 2nd horse • Strap missing from 2nd horse • Stripe missing from helmet of 4th rider
- Arms of top of last rider on right changed color • Hoof of last horse on right missing

Safe landing

Complete this puzzle and jump it up a level.

WIZARD

1. ☐

2. ☐

3. ☐

4. ☐

5. ☐

6. ☐

7. ☐

8. ☐

9. ☐

4 mins 10 secs

WIZARD

ANSWERS

Poster on wall missing • Light on wall missing • Chimney missing
Skateboard bigger • Window missing • Door different color
Shadow of skater missing • Button on skater's pocket missing • Knot on wood on ramp missing

Make a home

How are your DIY skills?

WIZARD

1. ☐
2. ☐
3. ☐
4. ☐
5. ☐
6. ☐
7. ☐
8. ☐
9. ☐

4 mins 10 secs

WIZARD

ANSWERS

• Knot on wood front of pic missing • Writing on piece of wood under boy's foot missing
• Middle button on boy's shirt missing • Wooden support above boy's head missing • Shirt button of man missing
• Ring on woman's right-hand missing • Man's fingers behind woman's back missing
• Work bench missing • Horizontal support missing right of pic

Odd one out

Which picture is different?

A. ☐

B. ☐

C. ☐

D. ☐

50 secs

A

B

C

D

WIZARD

ANSWER: C - Yellow pack missing

Odd one out

Can you spot the odd one out?
Or will it drive you mad?

A. ☐
B. ☐
C. ☐
D. ☐

40 secs

A

B

C

D

ANSWER: D - Driver's head missing

Al fresco dining

Finding these changes is a picnic.

WIZARD

1. ☐
2. ☐
3. ☐
4. ☐
5. ☐
6. ☐
7. ☐
8. ☐
9. ☐

4 mins 10 secs

WIZARD

ANSWERS

• Strut in chair on left missing • Hand on left, bracelet missing • Man's shirt button missing
• Woman in pink, hair parting missing • Stripe in glass woman in pink holding changed • Woman with green shirt pocket missing
• Woman in blue necklace pendant missing • Yellow napkin changed color • Salad bowl missing salad & tongs

What's new?

It's time to contemplate these changes.

1. ☐
2. ☐
3. ☐
4. ☐
5. ☐
6. ☐
7. ☐
8. ☐
9. ☐

4 mins 5 secs

ANSWERS

• Large crack in pillar missing • Extra column in alcove • Leaf on ground missing
• Extra fold at bottom of monk's gown • Part of trees in background missing • Monk's ear bigger
• Alcove on right missing • Block in alcove missing • Roof between pillars missing

Piggyback

Do you need some help? Or can you spot the all changes?

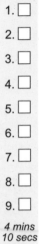

1. ☐
2. ☐
3. ☐
4. ☐
5. ☐
6. ☐
7. ☐
8. ☐
9. ☐

4 mins
10 secs

ANSWERS

- Log behind woman's shoulder missing • Seams on woman's jeans missing • Fence missing
- Man's cap different color • Boy's shoe missing • Red tab in man's pocket missing
- Man's t-shirt longer • Stripe on boy's shirt missing • Boy's thumb missing

WIZARD

The lost city

Find your way in the lost city of the Incas.

1. ☐

2. ☐

3. ☐

4. ☐

5. ☐

6. ☐

7. ☐

8. ☐

9. ☐

4 mins 20 secs

ANSWERS

• Strap on man's bag missing • Woman's boot missing • Strap on woman's top missing
• Man's bag different color • Tree in ruins missing • Top of mountain taller
• Doorway filled in • Extra building in large field • Building at base of mountain missing

WIZARD

Bird's eye view

You'll need an eagle eye for the Know It All level.
There are 11 differences.

★★

1. ☐
2. ☐
3. ☐
4. ☐
5. ☐
6. ☐
7. ☐
8. ☐
9. ☐
10. ☐
11. ☐

5 mins 10 secs

KNOW IT ALL

ANSWERS

- Window in tower missing • Bird missing • Cross on dome missing
- Man's ring missing • Woman's shoe strap missing • Man's trousers different color
- Pigeon on right has foot missing • Woman's belt missing • Man in pink shirt in background missing
- Statue missing from top of arch • Shape missing from roof on building to left

The eye of the beholder

This picture requires the fine art of observation.

ANSWERS

• Post in water on left missing • Duck to left of woman missing • Woman's cardigan changed color • Some of painting missing • Jar on bench missing • Large reflection in water under woman missing • Some paint in mixers missing • Water in jar changed color • Branch hanging down missing • Man walking on opposite bank missing • Large branch on tree right-hand side missing

1. ☐ 2. ☐ 3. ☐ 4. ☐ 5. ☐ 6. ☐ 7. ☐ 8. ☐ 9. ☐ 10. ☐ 11. ☐

5 mins 10 secs

Cityscape

All cities look the same at night. Or do they?

ANSWERS

• Boat on left-hand side missing • Crack in pavement on left missing • Screw on bench left-hand missing • Buoy in middle of picture missing • Leg on right-hand bench missing • Strut in railing middle of pic missing • Light in middle of bridge missing • Light on top of left-hand building missing • Floor of tall building darkened • Light on tall building right-hand side missing • Building on right-hand side missing

★★

1. ☐
2. ☐
3. ☐
4. ☐
5. ☐
6. ☐
7. ☐
8. ☐
9. ☐
10. ☐
11. ☐

5 mins

Out of order

Put this picture in the right order

50 secs

A

B

C

D

ANSWER: D, A, B, C

Out of order

What is the correct order for this picture perfect view?

A

B

C

D

ANSWER: B, C, A, D

A place of worship

There's a lot to discover at this famous Cathedral in Spain.

★★

1. ☐
2. ☐
3. ☐
4. ☐
5. ☐
6. ☐
7. ☐
8. ☐
9. ☐
10. ☐
11. ☐

5 mins 5 secs

ANSWERS

• Crane on right missing • Oval window on left missing
• Statue on triangular arch missing • Cross on left spire missing • Bridge between left-hand spires missing
• Shield on left-hand crane missing • Cable on tallest crane missing • Inscription on second spire from left missing
• Extra flower in foreground • Extra tower on right-hand side • Small window slits near center missing

Fountain of knowledge

There's more to this than meets the eye.

★★

1. ☐
2. ☐
3. ☐
4. ☐
5. ☐
6. ☐
7. ☐
8. ☐
9. ☐
10. ☐
11. ☐

5 mins 5 secs

KNOW IT ALL

ANSWERS

• Gold face missing • Fish nostril missing • Street lamps missing
• Crest on building missing • Chimney on right missing • Inset on wall missing
• Top of fountain missing • Scythe in cherub's hand missing • Cherub's gold cloak missing
• Pineapple in statue's arm missing • Person in blue shirt on right missing

Venetian blind?

Can you see all 11 changes?

ANSWERS

• Banner on bridge different color • Chimney missing on building on right • Boat under bridge bigger • Window missing on orange building • Extra chimney on white building • Extra mooring pole on left • Statue on left of bridge missing • Woman sitting on steps missing • Green graffiti on black door missing • Extra window on roof • TV aerial on left missing

★★

1. ☐
2. ☐
3. ☐
4. ☐
5. ☐
6. ☐
7. ☐
8. ☐
9. ☐
10. ☐
11. ☐

5 mins 10 secs

All aboard!

Join this London bus on a mystery tour.

1. ☐
2. ☐
3. ☐
4. ☐
5. ☐
6. ☐
7. ☐
8. ☐
9. ☐
10. ☐
11. ☐

5 mins 5 secs

ANSWERS

• Number on bus missing • Plate in corner of radiator grill missing • Indicator on bus missing • Hour hand on clock face missing • Window on Big Ben roof missing • Spire on top of Big Ben missing • Bus in background missing • Bus headlight missing • Wiper on bus window missing • Man by railings missing • Tall window in tower missing

Rooms with a view

Get a window on reality with this picture.

KNOW IT ALL

ANSWERS

• Wake behind main boat missing • 3rd water spout from boat missing
• Window support from upper deck of boat missing • American flag missing • Decoration on 4th window above arch missing
• 4th window under dome missing • 1st set of aerials on black tower missing • 3rd column on building above front of boat missing
• Blind up instead of down on 5th floor of building above boat • Cloak missing from clock tower • Balcony missing from tower block right of picture

★★

1. ☐
2. ☐
3. ☐
4. ☐
5. ☐
6. ☐
7. ☐
8. ☐
9. ☐
10. ☐
11. ☐

5 mins 5 secs

Lost in the woods

It's not easy, but you can find your way out.

★★

1. ☐
2. ☐
3. ☐
4. ☐
5. ☐
6. ☐
7. ☐
8. ☐
9. ☐
10. ☐
11. ☐

5 mins 10 secs

KNOW IT ALL

ANSWERS

- Knot on root trunk missing left • Root at front missing
- Leaf missing on trunk • Falling leaf missing near woman's head
- Stiching on boot missing • Stiching on left shoulder missing • Bracelet missing • Ring missing
- Zip missing • Earring missing • Falling leaf top of picture far right missing

Walk like an Egyptian

The pyramids hold many secrets.

1. ☐
2. ☐
3. ☐
4. ☐
5. ☐
6. ☐
7. ☐
8. ☐
9. ☐
10. ☐
11. ☐

5 mins 10 secs

ANSWERS

- Red knot on camel's nose missing • Loop under camel's mouth missing
- Clasp on strap under neck missing • Red rope missing around neck • Rock under camel's head missing
- 3rd pyramid missing • Small pyramid missing • Handle on seat missing • Blue tassle missing
- Red triangle on blanket re colored • Mat on back recolored

The leaning tower

It's time to even up your score.

ANSWERS

• Cross on top of dome missing • Circular window in arch missing
• Chimney on roof missing • Cloud on left missing • Woman in pink on steps missing • Gargoyle on right wall of church missing
• Diamond shape in arch at base of tower missing • Window on cream building missing
• Extra window in ground floor of church • Red fire hydrant missing • Flag missing

★★

1. ☐
2. ☐
3. ☐
4. ☐
5. ☐
6. ☐
7. ☐
8. ☐
9. ☐
10. ☐
11. ☐

5 mins 5 secs

The Great Wall

You may hit a wall on this one, but keep going.

★★

1. ☐
2. ☐
3. ☐
4. ☐
5. ☐
6. ☐
7. ☐
8. ☐
9. ☐
10. ☐
11. ☐

5 mins 5 secs

ANSWERS

• Window on left-hand side of turret missing • Middle part of rampart missing
• Boy in black halfway down missing • Drainpipe left-hand side of wall missing • Red & white flag missing near middle
• Flag on right-hand edge of wall missing • Pipe down right-hand side of wall missing • White & red flag missing left-hand side of wall
• Man in white & black missing at bottom of stair • Red flag at bottom recoloured • Blue flag left-hand side recoloured

Out of order

Put the pieces of this picture in the right order.

★★

40 secs

A

B

C

D

ANSWER: B, C, D, A

Out of order

What's the correct order?
See if you can beat the clock.

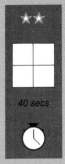

★★

40 secs

A B

C D

ANSWER: B, D, A, C

On safari

Join the tourists and spot what's changed.

★★

1. ☐
2. ☐
3. ☐
4. ☐
5. ☐
6. ☐
7. ☐
8. ☐
9. ☐
10. ☐
11. ☐

5 mins 10 secs

ANSWERS

• Clouds missing • Elephant missing • Branch in middle of tree missing
• Elephant's tusk missing • Wing mirror missing • Red bar on front of jeep different color
• Bush missing • Rear bumper on jeep missing • Headlight missing • Ridge on bonnet missing • White band on hat missing

Girl next door

It's getting harder. The Mastermind level has 15 changes.

MASTERMIND

★★

1. ☐
2. ☐
3. ☐
4. ☐
5. ☐
6. ☐
7. ☐
8. ☐
9. ☐
10. ☐
11. ☐
12. ☐
13. ☐
14. ☐
15. ☐

5 mins
10 secs

ANSWERS

• Number missing on door • Beads different color • Door handle missing
• Spot on dress missing • Suede boot higher up leg • Letterbox larger
• Button on yellow cardigan missing • Number 3 upside down • Part of frame in left window missing
• Pocket seam on jeans missing • Girl's hand on wall missing • Part of drain cover missing
• Mortar in bricks on left arch missing • Spot on dress different color • Mark in paint on left door missing

MASTERMIND

Snowed under

Find the 15 changes in this picture.

MASTERMIND

★★

1. ☐
2. ☐
3. ☐
4. ☐
5. ☐
6. ☐
7. ☐
8. ☐
9. ☐
10. ☐
11. ☐
12. ☐
13. ☐
14. ☐
15. ☐

5 mins 20 secs

ANSWERS

• Shape on snowboard different • Cord on girl's hood missing • White line on brown jacket missing
• Zip on girl's pocket missing • Strap on snowboard missing • Color of girl's goggles different
• Leaf pattern on coat missing • Color of sleeve holding board different • Red band on jacket different color
• Toggle on blue hood missing • Black helmet larger • Tassle on girl's hat larger
• Ridge on man's helmet missing • Red logo on girl's goggle strap missing • White cord on man's hood missing

Paris Metro

Take a trip on the Metro and see what's changed.

★★

1. ☐
2. ☐
3. ☐
4. ☐
5. ☐
6. ☐
7. ☐
8. ☐
9. ☐
10. ☐
11. ☐
12. ☐
13. ☐
14. ☐
15. ☐

5 mins 5 secs

MASTERMIND

ANSWERS

- Number 14 missing • Street sign on wall missing • Camera on wall missing
- Red light missing • Letter 'O' in Metropolitain upside down • Pillars on balcony missing
- Painting on sign different color • Arrow on street sign missing • Rubbish sack more vibrant green
- Bollard missing behind scooter • Pedal on scooter missing • Handle on scooter missing
- Painting on billboard larger • Line on building missing • Part of stand on scooter missing

Today's bargain

What's on offer on these market stalls in Morocco?

ANSWERS

• Melon missing far left on stall • No. 55 missing on front of box far left
• Decoration missing under 1st stall • 3rd star missing on 1st stall canopy • Bunch of bananas missing right of 1st stall
• Stripe on boy's right arm missing • Spindle front wheel of bike missing • Wheel under 2nd stall missing
• Orange fruit missing front of 2nd stall • 1st bunch of bananas missing 3rd stall • 1st star on canopy missing on 3rd stall
• Bike wheel missing far right • Part of mesh missing from wall • Satellite dish missing • Window on far right top wall missing

1. ☐ 2. ☐ 3. ☐ 4. ☐ 5. ☐ 6. ☐ 7. ☐ 8. ☐ 9. ☐ 10. ☐ 11. ☐ 12. ☐ 13. ☐ 14. ☐ 15. ☐

5 mins 10 secs

School's out

Notice any changes in this group of students?

★★

1. ☐
2. ☐
3. ☐
4. ☐
5. ☐
6. ☐
7. ☐
8. ☐
9. ☐
10. ☐
11. ☐
12. ☐
13. ☐
14. ☐
15. ☐

5 mins 10 secs

MASTERMIND

ANSWERS

- Branch of tree missing • Boy with stripes headphone cable missing
- Arm of girl's glasses missing • Part of pattern on light blue bag missing • Girl on left earring missing
- Girl on right dress different color • White strap missing on girl's shoe • Boy's tie different color
- Seam missing on girl's jeans • Chimney missing behind girl's head • Base of bench leg on left missing
- Gap between bench slats missing • Crease in front of girl's white top missing
- Girl with black trousers belt missing • Gold clasp on black bag missing

Odd one out

Can you spot the odd one out in under 10 seconds?

★★

A. ☐

B. ☐

C. ☐

D. ☐

10 secs

A

B

C

D

ANSWER: D - Line on bow of kayak missing

Odd one out

All the fun of the fair. Which one is different?

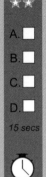

A

B

C

D

★★

A. ☐

B. ☐

C. ☐

D. ☐

15 secs

ANSWER: B - Chair missing

A London hotspot

Trafalgar Square has lots happening. Can you see the changes?

MASTERMIND

ANSWERS

• Drain cover at front missing • Man on horse on plinth missing
• Window missing 2nd from right 1st building • South African flag missing • Foliage at top missing
• Woman on left missing • Top circular window missing on first tower middle building • Union Jack missing
• Woman sitting by fountain in black missing • Joint in fountain wall missing • Fountain on right missing
• Boy under Nelson's column missing • 1st concrete bollard on right missing • Head of Nelson missing • Chimney stack on right missing

★★

1. ☐
2. ☐
3. ☐
4. ☐
5. ☐
6. ☐
7. ☐
8. ☐
9. ☐
10. ☐
11. ☐
12. ☐
13. ☐
14. ☐
15. ☐

5 mins 10 secs

Jet-setter

Can you see all the changes before take off?

★★

1. ☐
2. ☐
3. ☐
4. ☐
5. ☐
6. ☐
7. ☐
8. ☐
9. ☐
10. ☐
11. ☐
12. ☐
13. ☐
14. ☐
15. ☐

5 mins 10 secs

ANSWERS

- Window far left missing • 2nd window missing • 2nd step missing
- Zip on suitcase missing • Strap on left shoe missing • 2nd button on trouser missing
- Ring on right-hand missing • Jacket changed color • Rivet missing on right-hand pocket
- Zip missing on jacket • Top of shirt missing • Reflection missing in sunglasses
- Right earring missing • Center of wheel missing • Stripe on engine missing

Out of order

What's the correct order for this New York scene?

★★

30 secs

A

B

C

D

ANSWER: A, D, B, C

★★

1. ☐
2. ☐
3. ☐
4. ☐
5. ☐
6. ☐
7. ☐
8. ☐
9. ☐
10. ☐
11. ☐
12. ☐
13. ☐
14. ☐
15. ☐

5 mins 10 secs

MASTERMIND

ANS

• Archway on left of building missing • Small … on left-hand side
• Square above doorway arch missing • Square in 1st column … • Boat hook far right missing
• Top of third light missing • Square on right-hand side colum… in brickwork middle missing
• Crucifix support on 1st dome missing • Color change… anged on 3rd dome
• Crucifix missing on 4th dome • Square changed col… missing far right

Party trick

Bobbing for apples is not easy, neither is this picture puzzle.

MASTERMIND

ANSWERS

• Spot on dog costume missing • Lamp on house missing • Button on brown pocket missing
• Rocket on badge on orange suit missing • Girl's headscarf different color • Apple in girl's mouth larger
• Blue flower on girl's poncho different color • Toggle on fireman's jacket missing • Web on lilac dress missing
• Extra apple in barrel • Shutter on window missing • Part of lattice on lilac dress missing
• Watch strap on girl's arm missing • Black stripe on girl's skirt missing • Strut on fence in front of house missing

★★

1.
2.
3.
4.
5.
6.
7.
8.
9.
10.
11.
12.
13.
14.
15.

5 mins 5 secs

Yeah!

You will get a cheer if you complete this puzzle in time.

★★

1. ☐
2. ☐
3. ☐
4. ☐
5. ☐
6. ☐
7. ☐
8. ☐
9. ☐
10. ☐
11. ☐
12. ☐
13. ☐
14. ☐
15. ☐

5 mins 10 secs

ANSWERS

• Red glove different color • Stripe on shirt missing • Reflection in car window missing
• Tassle on top pom-pom missing • Number 1 on glove missing • Love heart on girl's necklace missing
• White paint on man's neck missing • Girl's hoop earring missing • Man's collar different color
• Girl's ring missing • Pocket on girl's jeans missing • Paint on man's cheek different color
• Paint on girl's cheek missing • Seam on girl's jeans in background missing • Tail light on black car different color

MASTERMIND

Odd one out

Can you see which picture is different?

★★

A. ☐

B. ☐

C. ☐

D. ☐

50 secs

A

B

C

D

ANSWER: C - Piece of snow in top left missing

Odd one out

Which picture is different?

★★

A. ☐

B. ☐

C. ☐

D. ☐

15 secs

A

B

C

D

ANSWER: A - Stripe on shorts different color

Masked ball

Can you uncover the 15 changes?

MASTERMIND

ANSWERS

• Tower in background missing • Fabric in gondola different color
• Beam in fence on dock missing • Pleat in dress missing • Mark under man's nose missing
• Brooch on man's fur collar missing • Part of woman's necklace missing • Frond in woman's hat missing
• Pole in water missing • Line in woman's ruff missing • Woman's lips bigger
• Claw on man's glove missing • Rose different color • Lamp on left missing • Shape on bow of gondola different

1. ☐
2. ☐
3. ☐
4. ☐
5. ☐
6. ☐
7. ☐
8. ☐
9. ☐
10. ☐
11. ☐
12. ☐
13. ☐
14. ☐
15. ☐

5 mins 10 secs

Out of order

This photo is all mixed up.
What is the correct order?

★★

30 secs

A B

C D

ANSWER: C, D, A, B